I0817204

SPORTS SUPERSTARS

By Kevin Frederickson

Kaleidoscope
Minneapolis, MN

Your Front Row Seat to the Games

This edition is co-published by agreement between Kaleidoscope and World Book, Inc.

Kaleidoscope Publishing, Inc.
6012 Blue Circle Drive
Minnetonka, MN 55343 U.S.A.

World Book, Inc.
180 North LaSalle St., Suite 900
Chicago IL 60601 U.S.A.

Kaleidoscope ISBNs
978-1-64519-048-6 (library bound)
978-1-64494-205-5 (paperback)
978-1-64519-149-0 (ebook)

World Book ISBN
978-0-7166-4352-4 (library bound)

Library of Congress Control Number
2019940067

Printed in the United States of America.

TABLE OF CONTENTS

CHAPTER 1

A True Warrior

The ball is loose. Steph Curry grabs it near the hoop. The Golden State Warriors point guard **dribbles**. But he's stuck. Cleveland Cavaliers defender Kevin Love is in his face. Love is shuffling his feet to stay with Curry. His hands are high in the air.

Curry tries backing up. But time is running out. The **shot clock** says 4.5 seconds. It's Game 2 of the 2018 National Basketball Association (NBA) Finals. The Warriors are on their way to a win. But Curry wants more.

FUN FACT

Curry was one of three former NBA Most Valuable Player (MVP) winners playing in this game.

Steph Curry celebrates a basket in Game 2 of the 2018 NBA Finals.

Curry brings the ball up the floor in Game 2.

Curry keeps dribbling. He moves back. Now he's behind the **three-point line**. Love puts his hand next to Curry's face. Curry moves even farther back. Less than a second remains on the shot clock. Finally, Curry jumps. The ball sits in his hands. Then he snaps his wrist. The ball floats through the air. The buzzer sounds. It swishes through the hoop. The TV announcer screams in excitement.

"He knocks it down!" he says.

Curry made nine three-pointers that night. No player had ever made that many in an NBA Finals game.

The Warriors win the next game. If they win one more, they're NBA champions. The Cavaliers players follow Curry all over the court in Game 4. They stand as close as to him they can. They don't want to give him any room to shoot.

But Curry continues to score. Later, Curry jumps into the air outside the three-point line. He bumps into the Cavaliers defender. Curry shoots with a flick of his right wrist. The ball swishes through the hoop. The fans ooh and ah.

Curry led the Warriors with 37 points in that game. Golden State won the game and the 2018 championship. Curry helped make it happen. He's one of the best three-point shooters in NBA history.

Curry holds the championship trophy at the team's celebration in Oakland in 2018.

CAREER STATS

Through the 2018–19 season

GAMES PLAYED	694
POINTS SCORED	16,315
ASSISTS	4,588
STEALS	1,200
THREE-POINT PERCENTAGE	.436

CHAPTER 2

Steph grew up watching his dad, Dell (30), play in the NBA.

A Rare Talent

Steph is standing near a huge NBA **logo**. He is at center court of the Charlotte Coliseum in Charlotte, North Carolina. A brown leather ball sits in his hand. He puts up a shot. It bounces off the glass and in. Swish! The ball goes through the net and lands on the floor. His father cheers.

Steph did this when he was just a few years old. He was born on March 14, 1988, in Akron, Ohio. He watched his father, Dell Curry, play for the Charlotte Hornets. Steph and his brother shot hoops with their dad before games.

Steph stands much shorter than some of his teammates at Charlotte Christian School. He's less than six feet (1.8 m) tall. But his talent stands out. He dribbles down the floor. He stops his dribbling just outside the three-point line. Everyone else keeps running toward the hoop. Steph is all alone. He bends his knees and attempts a three-pointer. It goes in. He runs back down the court.

Not many colleges wanted Steph. They thought he was too short. He went to tiny Davidson College. Steph led Davidson to the third round of the 2008 NCAA Tournament.

FUN FACT

Steph was named Most Outstanding Player in the Midwest region of the tournament.

Steph led Davidson to its best-ever performance at the NCAA Tournament in 2008.

Where Curry Has Been

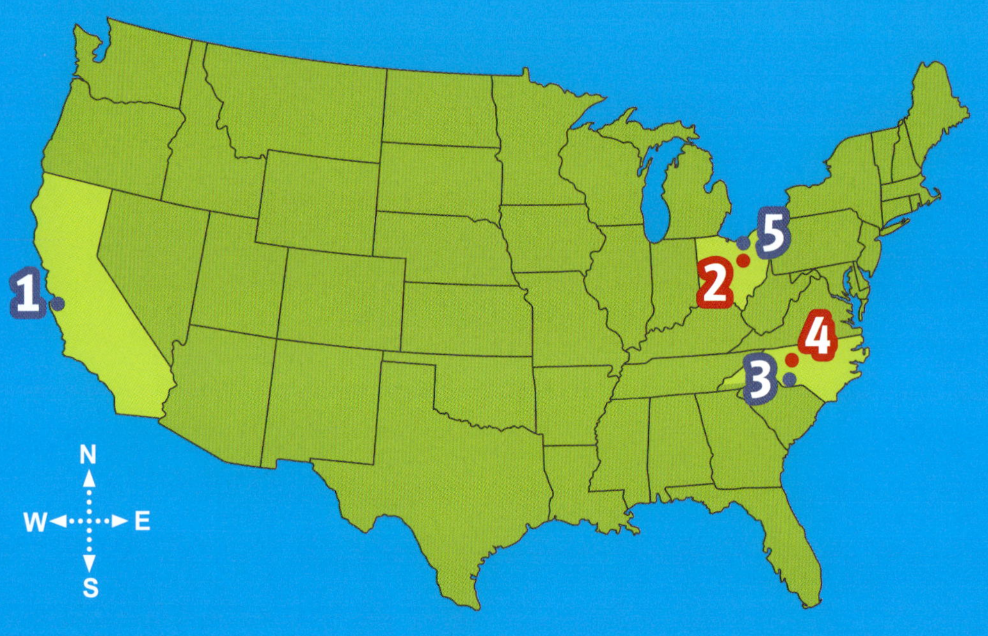

1 **San Francisco, California:** Where Curry plays with the Golden State Warriors.

2 **Akron, Ohio:** Curry was born here.

3 **Charlotte, North Carolina:** Curry grew up here while his father played for the Hornets.

4 **Davidson, North Carolina:** Curry played college basketball here.

5 **Cleveland, Ohio:** Curry won his first NBA championship here.

Steph runs down the left side of the floor. His teammate has the ball. Steph runs a few steps ahead and gets the pass. He dribbles toward the basket. It looks like he's going in on the left side. Then he dips underneath the hoop. He bounces the ball off the right side of the backboard. It goes in. Davidson fans jump out of their seats. Steph pumps his fist.

Davidson **upset** the University of Wisconsin. Davidson became well-known with Steph on the team. He was good enough in college to go on to the NBA.

FUN FACT

Davidson was one of the smallest schools in the tournament, with approximately 1,700 students.

Steph returned to Davidson for his junior season and led the nation in scoring.

CHAPTER 3

Helping Those in Need

Curry dribbles up the floor. He's moving very quickly. His teammates run toward the hoop. He stops behind the three-point line. He goes into his shooting motion. The ball flies out of his hand. The ball goes straight through the hoop. Swish!

Curry has made thousands of three-pointers in his career. Each one has meaning. Every time Curry hits one of these shots, three nets are donated to kids in Africa. These nets help keep mosquitoes away. These bugs can carry diseases.

Curry scores while playing in a charity basketball game in 2011.

FUN FACT
Curry's younger brother Seth made his NBA debut in 2014.

Daughter Riley is Curry's oldest child.

Curry stands with a group of kids. He is wearing a white shirt. It says, "Nothing But Nets." He is in Africa. Curry is there delivering nets to kids. In 2013, he donated 816 nets to kids. They hug him to say thank you. It's one of the things Curry does to help others.

Curry loves spending time with his family. He sits down near his wife, Ayesha. His kids come running over. Riley was born in 2012. She sits on her dad's lap. She did that as a two-year-old at the NBA Finals. This happened during a **press conference**. She laughed and had fun. Everyone was talking about Riley.

GETTING GIRLS TO PLAY

A young girl went to the store. She was looking for new shoes for basketball. She loved Curry. She wanted to buy the same shoes he wears. But the store did not have his shoes for girls. The girl was sad. She wrote a note to Curry. She asked why his shoes weren't for both boys and girls. Curry saw the letter. He was shocked. He wrote back to her. He said he was sorry. He made sure his shoes were now available for both boys and girls.

CAREER TIMELINE

1988

March 14, 1988
Steph Curry is born in Akron, Ohio.

2006

November 10, 2006
Curry makes his debut with Davidson College.

2007

March 15, 2007
Curry plays in his first NCAA Tournament game.

2008

March 28, 2008
Curry scores 33 points and helps Davidson beat Wisconsin in the NCAA Tournament.

2009

June 25, 2009
Curry is drafted by the Golden State Warriors with the seventh overall pick.

2015

May 4, 2015
Curry wins his first NBA Most Valuable Player (MVP) award.

2015

June 16, 2015
Curry helps the Warriors to the 2015 NBA championship.

2016

May 10, 2016
Curry wins his second MVP award in a row.

2018

June 8, 2018
Curry wins his third NBA championship.

His son Ryan was born in 2015. Another son, Canon, is with Ayesha. He was born in 2018. They all spend most of their free time together. Curry takes video of the kids and posts it on Instagram. Fans love seeing Curry's family.

Curry and his wife, Ayesha, met in a church youth group when they were teenagers.

CHAPTER 4

Getting to the Top

Two **trophies** sit on a table. Curry smiles nearby in his blue suit. He stands next to former NBA player Steve Nash. Nash is there to give Curry his second NBA MVP award.

Curry's family and teammates sit in the crowd. They clap and cheer when Nash hands the trophy to Curry. Curry holds both trophies in the air. He has already become one of the greatest players in NBA history.

Fans can buy basketball shoes that Curry helped design.

Curry poses with his second MVP trophy in 2016.

It's the 2018 NBA Playoffs. Curry bounces the ball quickly down the floor. Teammate Draymond Green is open. Curry passes the ball to Green. Green is standing in the corner. He quickly shoots a three-pointer. It goes in. Curry gives a high-five to Green. Curry does more than just shoot for the Warriors. He's also the point guard. He makes good passes to teammates so they can score.

And the Warriors do a lot of scoring. With Curry, they run an incredible offense. Later in the game, the ball is loose on the floor. Players from the Warriors and Houston Rockets run after it. Eventually, Curry picks it up. He dribbles slowly up the floor. The players run to their positions. Curry dribbles in the center of the floor. He's a foot behind the three-point line.

Curry makes a pass without looking during a 2016 game.

Curry celebrates in front of Warriors fans in Game 1 of the 2018 NBA Finals.

Houston's James Harden stands right in front of Curry. Curry tries to dribble around Harden. But Harden stays in front of him no matter what. Ten seconds go by. Curry is still dribbling. Curry decides to pick up the ball. He throws up a shot. The ball swishes through the hoop. The fans rise to their feet. Curry runs backward. He stops and moves his shoulders. It's his famous shimmy dance. Curry often does this after making three-pointers. That includes this three-pointer against Houston.

The Warriors went on to win the NBA title. It was their second in a row. And it was the third one for Curry. He had made it to the top. And he brought the Warriors with him.

BEYOND THE BOOK

After reading the book, it's time to think about what you learned. Try the following exercises to jumpstart your ideas.

THINK

THAT'S NEWS TO ME. Think about the 2018 NBA Finals. Find an article online about that series. Read more about the other games in the series. What were other important moments that helped the Warriors win?

CREATE

PRIMARY SOURCES. Primary sources are documents or sources that were made at the time of an event. They might include interviews, photos, and videos. Create a list of primary sources that talk about Curry. What kinds of information could you learn from these sources?

SHARE

WHAT'S YOUR OPINION? Chapter Four says Curry is one of the greatest players in NBA history. Do you agree with that opinion? Tell a friend your opinion and provide evidence. Does your friend find the argument convincing?

GROW

REAL-LIFE RESEARCH. What kind of place could you go to learn more about basketball and Curry? What are some other things you could learn by visiting this place?

RESEARCH NINJA

Visit www.ninjaresearcher.com/0486 to learn how to take your research skills and book report writing to the next level!

RESEARCH

DIGITAL LITERACY TOOLS

SEARCH LIKE A PRO

Learn about how to use search engines to find useful websites.

FACT OR FAKE?

Discover how you can tell a trusted website from an untrustworthy resource.

TEXT DETECTIVE

Explore how to zero in on the information you need most.

SHOW YOUR WORK

Research responsibly—learn how to cite sources.

WRITE

GET TO THE POINT

Learn how to express your main ideas.

PLAN OF ATTACK

Learn prewriting exercises and create an outline.

DOWNLOADABLE REPORT FORMS

Further Resources

BOOKS

Abdo, Kenny. *Stephen Curry*. Abdo Zoom, 2018.

Raum, Elizabeth. *Stephen Curry*. Amicus, 2020.

Smith, Brett. *Stephen Curry*. Abdo, 2018.

WEBSITES

FACTSURFER

Factsurfer.com gives you a safe, fun way to find more information.

1. Go to www.factsurfer.com.
2. Enter “Steph Curry” into the search box and click 🔍.
3. Select your book cover to see a list of related websites.

Glossary

dribbles: A player dribbles when he bounces the basketball off the floor. Curry dribbles the ball up the floor when he plays point guard.

logo: A logo is a graphic that represents a company or team. Curry wears the Golden State Warriors logo on his jersey.

press conference: A press conference is when players meet with reporters to talk about a game or practice. Curry has a press conference after most of his playoff games.

shot clock: Some levels of basketball use a shot clock to give a team a certain amount of time to shoot. The NBA shot clock lasts 24 seconds.

three-point line: The three-point line is an arc on the court that defines where a player needs to shoot to make it count for three points. Curry took a shot with his toes just behind the three-point line.

trophies: Trophies are statues that teams and players get for winning something. Curry has won two NBA MVP trophies.

upset: An upset is when one team unexpectedly beats a stronger team. The Davidson Wildcats upset the Wisconsin Badgers in 2008.

Index

PHOTO CREDITS

The images in this book are reproduced through the courtesy of: Steve Dykes/AP Images, front cover (center); Ben Margot/AP Images, front cover (right), pp. 3, 5, 23, 26; Aaron Amat/Shutterstock Images, p. 4, 20 (right); Marcio Jose Sanchez/AP Images, pp. 6, 8; Ververidis Vasilis/Shutterstock Images, p. 7; Red Line Editorial, pp. 9 (chart), 14, 20; Tony Dejak/AP Images, p. 9 (Steph Curry); Fred Jewell/AP Images, p. 10; digidreamgrafix/Shutterstock Images, p. 11; Al Sermeno Photography/Shutterstock Images, p. 12; Chuck Burton/AP Images, p. 13; Brett Flashnick/AP Images, p. 15; Sun_Shine/Shutterstock Images, p. 16; Jeff Chiu/AP Images, p. 17; Kathy Hutchins/Shutterstock Images, p. 18; Gosteva/Shutterstock Images, pp. 20 (left), 22; Tinseltown/Shutterstock Images, p. 21; David Blair/Cal Sport Media/AP Images, pp. 24–25; mipan/Shutterstock Images, p. 27.

ABOUT THE AUTHOR

Kevin Frederickson is a freelance writer and editor from Ohio. He lives near Cincinnati with his golden doodle, Max.